LUNAR
living

2 0 2 3
WEEKLY PLANNER
JULY 2022—DECEMBER 2023

ROCK
POINT

2023 YEAR AT A GLANCE

JANUARY

S	M	T	W	T	F	S
1	2	3	4	5	6	7
8	9	10	11	12	13	14
15	16	17	18	19	20	21
22	23	24	25	26	27	28
29	30	31				

FEBRUARY

S	M	T	W	T	F	S
			1	2	3	4
5	6	7	8	9	10	11
12	13	14	15	16	17	18
19	20	21	22	23	24	25
26	27	28				

MARCH

S	M	T	W	T	F	S
			1	2	3	4
5	6	7	8	9	10	11
12	13	14	15	16	17	18
19	20	21	22	23	24	25
26	27	28	29	30	31	

APRIL

S	M	T	W	T	F	S
						1
2	3	4	5	6	7	8
9	10	11	12	13	14	15
16	17	18	19	20	21	22
23	24	25	26	27	28	29
30						

MAY

S	M	T	W	T	F	S
	1	2	3	4	5	6
7	8	9	10	11	12	13
14	15	16	17	18	19	20
21	22	23	24	25	26	27
28	29	30	31			

JUNE

S	M	T	W	T	F	S
				1	2	3
4	5	6	7	8	9	10
11	12	13	14	15	16	17
18	19	20	21	22	23	24
25	26	27	28	29	30	

JULY

S	M	T	W	T	F	S
						1
2	3	4	5	6	7	8
9	10	11	12	13	14	15
16	17	18	19	20	21	22
23	24	25	26	27	28	29
30	31					

AUGUST

S	M	T	W	T	F	S
		1	2	3	4	5
6	7	8	9	10	11	12
13	14	15	16	17	18	19
20	21	22	23	24	25	26
27	28	29	30	31		

SEPTEMBER

S	M	T	W	T	F	S
					1	2
3	4	5	6	7	8	9
10	11	12	13	14	15	16
17	18	19	20	21	22	23
24	25	26	27	28	29	30

OCTOBER

S	M	T	W	T	F	S
1	2	3	4	5	6	7
8	9	10	11	12	13	14
15	16	17	18	19	20	21
22	23	24	25	26	27	28
29	30	31				

NOVEMBER

S	M	T	W	T	F	S
			1	2	3	4
5	6	7	8	9	10	11
12	13	14	15	16	17	18
19	20	21	22	23	24	25
26	27	28	29	30		

DECEMBER

S	M	T	W	T	F	S
					1	2
3	4	5	6	7	8	9
10	11	12	13	14	15	16
17	18	19	20	21	22	23
24	25	26	27	28	29	30
31						

2024 YEAR AT A GLANCE

JANUARY
S	M	T	W	T	F	S
	1	2	3	4	5	6
7	8	9	10	11	12	13
14	15	16	17	18	19	20
21	22	23	24	25	26	27
28	29	30	31			

FEBRUARY
S	M	T	W	T	F	S
				1	2	3
4	5	6	7	8	9	10
11	12	13	14	15	16	17
18	19	20	21	22	23	24
25	26	27	28	29		

MARCH
S	M	T	W	T	F	S
					1	2
3	4	5	6	7	8	9
10	11	12	13	14	15	16
17	18	19	20	21	22	23
24	25	26	27	28	29	30
31						

APRIL
S	M	T	W	T	F	S
	1	2	3	4	5	6
7	8	9	10	11	12	13
14	15	16	17	18	19	20
21	22	23	24	25	26	27
28	29	30				

MAY
S	M	T	W	T	F	S
			1	2	3	4
5	6	7	8	9	10	11
12	13	14	15	16	17	18
19	20	21	22	23	24	25
26	27	28	29	30	31	

JUNE
S	M	T	W	T	F	S
						1
2	3	4	5	6	7	8
9	10	11	12	13	14	15
16	17	18	19	20	21	22
23	24	25	26	27	28	29
30						

JULY
S	M	T	W	T	F	S
	1	2	3	4	5	6
7	8	9	10	11	12	13
14	15	16	17	18	19	20
21	22	23	24	25	26	27
28	29	30	31			

AUGUST
S	M	T	W	T	F	S
				1	2	3
4	5	6	7	8	9	10
11	12	13	14	15	16	17
18	19	20	21	22	23	24
25	26	27	28	29	30	31

SEPTEMBER
S	M	T	W	T	F	S
1	2	3	4	5	6	7
8	9	10	11	12	13	14
15	16	17	18	19	20	21
22	23	24	25	26	27	28
29	30					

OCTOBER
S	M	T	W	T	F	S
		1	2	3	4	5
6	7	8	9	10	11	12
13	14	15	16	17	18	19
20	21	22	23	24	25	26
27	28	29	30	31		

NOVEMBER
S	M	T	W	T	F	S
					1	2
3	4	5	6	7	8	9
10	11	12	13	14	15	16
17	18	19	20	21	22	23
24	25	26	27	28	29	30

DECEMBER
S	M	T	W	T	F	S
1	2	3	4	5	6	7
8	9	10	11	12	13	14
15	16	17	18	19	20	21
22	23	24	25	26	27	28
29	30	31				

the eight phases

The demands of daily life can make you feel chaotic, ungrounded, and out of balance. This planner is designed to help you gain control over this whirlwind by providing the organization of a weekly planner while acknowledging the rhythms of our closest neighbor, the Moon. Represented by icons within the calendars, you'll find the four major phases for each month: the Full Moon, the First Quarter Moon, the New Moon, and the Third Quarter Moon. Moon Rituals open each month to offer you guidance and remind you of the balance the Moon's energy brings.

FULL MOON: A Full Moon is just as majestic as it sounds: full of light, full of power, and full of magic. Use these moonbeams to illuminate what is working— and what is not working—in your own life. Take the time to release anything that you are ready to let go of and to clear the space you need for any intentions that you are trying to manifest.

WAXING GIBBOUS: As the moon continues to grow in her light, she enters the Waxing Gibbous phase. The light of this moon is not a full circle yet, but it is more than half of a circle. As the moon prepares to enter her fullest state, this is a good time for you to make any adjustments and change your course of action as needed. This phase starts just after the First Quarter and continues until the Full Moon.

FIRST QUARTER: The moon enters her First Quarter phase when she is one quarter of the way through her lunar cycle and she appears perfectly illuminated on one half. This is the time to take action, meet challenges head-on, and be decisive. A good way to remember this is by looking at the perfect line of shadow down the moon's center: this is the moment to draw a firm line, boundary, or decision in your life and stick to it.

WAXING CRESCENT: Directly after the New Moon, the moon appears in the night sky as a thin crescent. As it grows, you should follow suit. This is a time for planting seeds for future growth, developing your intentions, or starting a new project. This phase starts just after the New Moon and lasts until the First Quarter Moon.

WANING GIBBOUS: As the Full Moon's light begins to lessen, she enters the Waning Gibbous phase. Share the light that you were gifted by the recent Full Moon. This is a time of grateful reflection, giving back, and acknowledging any benefits you may have received from the intention that you set. This phase starts just after the Full Moon and continues until the Third Quarter Moon.

THIRD QUARTER: As the moon slowly loses her glow and appears like a mirror image of the First Quarter Moon, the moon enters her Third Quarter phase (sometimes referred to as the Last Quarter Moon or Half Moon). As the moon releases her light, you should take this moment to release any deep emotions. Any negative emotions or anger should now be acknowledged so that they can be cleansed. This is a beautiful time to forgive yourself and others.

WANING CRESCENT: As the moon continues her cycle around the Earth, she becomes a tiny, bright sliver. This is known as her Waning Crescent phase. Just as the moon is preparing to enter her next cycle, so should you. This is a time to rest, recuperate, and ready yourself for the next phase in your life. This phase begins just after the Third Quarter Moon and continues until the New Moon.

NEW MOON: This moon, hidden beneath shadows and casting no reflection, is a time for new beginnings. Use this period of darkness to focus on things in your life that are waiting to be brought into the light. This is the best time to set clear, achievable, and specific intentions.

July 2022

NOTES	SUNDAY	MONDAY	TUESDAY
	3	4	5
		INDEPENDENCE DAY (US)	
	10	11	12
	17	18	19
	24	25	26
	31		

July 2022

WEDNESDAY	THURSDAY	FRIDAY	SATURDAY
		1 CANADA DAY (CAN)	2
6	7 ◖	8	9
13 ●	14	15	16
20 ◗	21	22	23
27	28 ○	29	30

June / July 2022

MONDAY (JUNE) 27

TUESDAY (JUNE) 28

WEDNESDAY (JUNE) 29

THURSDAY (JUNE) 30

FRIDAY
CANADA DAY (CAN) 1

SATURDAY 2

SUNDAY 3

July 2022

MONDAY
INDEPENDENCE DAY (US)

4

TUESDAY

5

WEDNESDAY

6

◖ THURSDAY

7

FRIDAY

8

SATURDAY

9

SUNDAY

10

BUCK MOON
July's Buck Moon is a time for growth and maturation—a time to claim your independence. You are called to recognize the freedom and authority you have in your life and to acknowledge the wisdom that you possess to confidently make your own decisions.

July 2022

MONDAY 11

TUESDAY 12

● **WEDNESDAY** 13

THURSDAY 14

FRIDAY
15

SATURDAY
16

SUNDAY
17

Speak the Buck Moon affirmation while
under the light of the Full Moon: *I can
overcome every obstacle in my life and I trust
that I can overcome any challenges ahead.*

MONDAY 18

TUESDAY 19

WEDNESDAY 20

THURSDAY 21

FRIDAY 22

SATURDAY 23

SUNDAY 24

"There's truths you
have to grow into."
—H.G. WELLS

July 2022

MONDAY 25

TUESDAY 26

WEDNESDAY 27

O **THURSDAY** 28

FRIDAY

29

SATURDAY

30

SUNDAY

31

To enjoy the benefits of nature without having to
venture into the wild, you can create a nature sounds
playlist. It has been scientifically proven that listening to
nature sounds lowers your blood pressure and decreases
cortisol, a stress hormone.

August
Sturgeon Moon

The Algonquins named this August moon after the abundance of sturgeon that would fill the lakes at this time of year. This moon is a reminder to be thankful for the abundance you have and to be patient for the beautiful things to come.

GRATITUDE GARLAND EXERCISE

What you need:

- Index cards
- Pen
- Hole punch
- Fishing line or red string

1. Sit somewhere comfortable and quiet. Breathe deeply to bring yourself into the present moment.

2. Take an index card and write something on it for which you are grateful. Remember: You want to focus on your financial life, so this can include your career, investments, debts you have paid, opportunities that have come your way, etc.

3. Repeat this for each index card.

4. Take each index card and, while oriented vertically, punch a hole in the top center.

5. Using your fishing line (as a nod to the sturgeon) or your red string, weave in and out of the index card holes, knotting the string at the top of each, until you have a garland with all 10 cards on it.

6. Hang this garland in the southeast area of your home, the section associated with wealth, to attract more abundance into your life.

August 2022

NOTES	SUNDAY	MONDAY	TUESDAY
		1 SUMMER BANK HOLIDAY (UK-SCT)	2
	7	8	9
	14	15	16
	21	22	23
	28	29 SUMMER BANK HOLIDAY (UK-ENG / NIR / WAL)	30

August 2022

WEDNESDAY	THURSDAY	FRIDAY	SATURDAY
3	4	◖ 5	6
10 ●	11	12	13
17	18	◗ 19	20
24	25	26 ○	27
31			

MONDAY
SUMMER BANK HOLIDAY (UK-SCT)

1

TUESDAY

2

WEDNESDAY

3

THURSDAY

4

FRIDAY

5

SATURDAY

6

SUNDAY

7

MONDAY 8

TUESDAY 9

WEDNESDAY 10

● **THURSDAY** 11

FRIDAY

12

SATURDAY

13

SUNDAY

14

STURGEON MOON

The Algonquins named this August moon after the abundance of sturgeon that would fill the lakes at this time of year. This moon is a reminder to be thankful for the abundance you have and to be patient for the beautiful things to come.

August 2022

MONDAY 15

TUESDAY 16

WEDNESDAY 17

THURSDAY 18

FRIDAY

19

SATURDAY

20

SUNDAY

21

Speak the Sturgeon Moon affirmation while under the light of the Full Moon: *I enjoy endless financial abundance and money flows to me easily and effortlessly.* Exhale. If you feel called, burn a dollar bill to release any past negative associations with money.

August 2022

MONDAY 22

TUESDAY 23

WEDNESDAY 24

THURSDAY 25

FRIDAY

26

O SATURDAY

27

SUNDAY

28

"Give a man a fish
and you feed him for a day;
teach a man to fish
and you feed him for a lifetime."
—MAIMONIDES

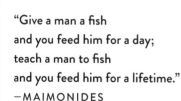

September
Corn Moon

A foundational staple of the Native American diet is maize, otherwise known as corn. This crop is ready for harvest each September and gave rise to this moon's name. Knowing what elements are foundational staples—not just in one's diet, but also in one's life—is the key to a thriving existence. This is a time for you to acknowledge the staples in your life and to identify the things, habits, and people you deem foundational and necessary. This is also a time to solidify all five necessary elements—physical, mental, emotional, spiritual, and social—of your self-care practice.

NEW MOON RITUAL

This intention-setting ritual will focus on using self-care to get you in alignment with your foundational staples.

SET THE SPACE

Incorporate visual representations of self-care into your space. You can display nutritious food, impactful books, a feel-good movie you love, candles, and photos of loved ones to remind yourself of all the different ways you show yourself care. Play meditative music or nature sounds to create a spa-like atmosphere. If you are using selenite, wear it as a necklace or display it somewhere visible. If you are saying a blessing before you begin, use self-care-centric words: health, mindset, harmony, care.

NOURISH YOUR BODY

Eat a couple handfuls of popcorn—a healthy snack appropriate for the Corn Moon.

SHIFT YOUR SPIRIT

To understand the benefits of self-care, you will first imagine what the most cared-for version of yourself is like.

HIGHEST SELF VISUALIZATION

1. Sit somewhere comfortable and close your eyes. Breathe deeply until you relax.

2. Imagine yourself 10 years from now. Imagine that you have developed an array of self-care habits and routines. Imagine that you are now your highest self—healthy, fulfilled, full of energy, and happy.

3. Take a close look at your highest self. What do you look like? How are you dressed? What is your career? Who are your friends? What does your daily life look like? How do you spend your free time? How does it feel to be this version of yourself?

CLOSING CEREMONY

Hug yourself while saying:
"I promise to care for you every single day."

September 2022

NOTES	SUNDAY	MONDAY	TUESDAY
	4	5	6
	FATHER'S DAY (AUS / NZ)	LABOR DAY (US) LABOUR DAY (CAN)	
	11 PATRIOT DAY (US) GRANDPARENTS' DAY (US)	12	13
	18	19	20
	25 ROSH HASHANAH (BEGINS AT SUNDOWN)	26	27

September 2022

WEDNESDAY	THURSDAY	FRIDAY	SATURDAY
	1	2	3
7	8	9	10
14	15	16	17
	FIRST DAY OF NATIONAL HISPANIC HERITAGE MONTH		
21	22	23	24
	FALL EQUINOX		
28	29	30	

MONDAY (AUGUST)
SUMMER BANK HOLIDAY (UK-ENG / NIR / WAL)

29

TUESDAY (AUGUST)

30

WEDNESDAY (AUGUST)

31

THURSDAY

1

FRIDAY

2

SATURDAY

3

SUNDAY
FATHER'S DAY (AUS / NZ)

4

MONDAY
LABOR DAY (US)
LABOUR DAY (CAN)

5

TUESDAY

6

WEDNESDAY

7

THURSDAY

8

FRIDAY

9

SATURDAY

10

SUNDAY
PATRIOT DAY (US)
GRANDPARENTS' DAY (US)

11

FIRST QUARTER MOON

This stage of the lunar cycle calls on your abilities
to be decisive, take action, and meet challenges.
To do this, your mind must be alert and clear.
Intellectual self-care is a beautiful way to cultivate
an efficient brain.

September 2022

MONDAY

12

TUESDAY

13

WEDNESDAY

14

THURSDAY
NATIONAL HISPANIC HERITAGE MONTH BEGINS

15

FRIDAY 16

SATURDAY 17

SUNDAY 18

CORN MOON CRYSTAL

Selenite is a translucent white stone that is connected with angelic realms and the moon, as it received its name from the Greek goddess of the moon, Selene. This crystal helps tie you to positive energy and feel spiritually rejuvenated.

September 2022

MONDAY 19

TUESDAY 20

WEDNESDAY 21

THURSDAY 22
FALL EQUINOX

FRIDAY 23

SATURDAY 24

○ SUNDAY 25
ROSH HASHANAH (BEGINS AT SUNDOWN)

"We become what we repeatedly do."
—SEAN COVEY

October
Hunter Moon

The manageable October temperatures provide a last chance to stock up on food before the long winter. This is how the Hunter Moon received its name—it coincides with the final hunt of the year. This is a time to strategically prepare for your future, fortify your spirit, and know you have what it takes to make it through difficult times. You are being called to develop coping mechanisms to carry you through the long winters in your own life.

WAXING CRESCENT MOON RITUAL

The Waxing Crescent calls you to start a project—ideally one that benefits the intention you set. One such project that focuses on emotional calm and stability is a *karesansui* or sand garden. The purpose of this calming garden full of sand that can be raked into a variety of patterns is to bring you to the present moment and create a sense of tranquility. It can be reproduced on a smaller scale so that you can have an indoor sand garden at home.

AIR PLANT SAND GARDEN

What you need:

- Tabletop-size shallow box or tray
- Essential oil
- Fine-grain sand
- An air plant
- Some small rocks or stones
- A small rake or your fingers

1. Place the shallow box on a solid surface.

2. Mix a few drops of essential oil into your sand, then fill the tray with it.

3. Add the air plant and the rocks or stones, placing them on top of the sand wherever you find them aesthetically pleasing.

4. To keep your air plant thriving, place the tray near a window with bright sunlight. Once a week, place the plant in room-temperature water for 10 minutes, dry it off, and place it back in the sand.

5. Using the rake or your fingers, draw lines, swirls, and patterns in the sand. You can then smooth the sand with your hand if you want to erase your lines.

6. Repeat this whenever you like for an immediately calming experience.

October 2022

NOTES	SUNDAY	MONDAY	TUESDAY
	◖ 2	3	4 YOM KIPPUR (BEGINS AT SUNDOWN)
	● 9 SUKKOT (BEGINS AT SUNDOWN)	10 INDIGENOUS PEOPLES' DAY (US) COLUMBUS DAY (US) THANKSGIVING DAY (CAN)	11
	16	◗ 17 SIMCHAT TORAH (BEGINS AT SUNDOWN)	18
	23	24 LABOUR DAY (NZ)	○ 25
	30	31 HALLOWEEN	

October 2022

WEDNESDAY	THURSDAY	FRIDAY	SATURDAY
			1
5	6	7	8
12	13	14	15
19	20	21	22
26	27	28	29

MONDAY (SEPTEMBER) 26

TUESDAY (SEPTEMBER) 27

WEDNESDAY (SEPTEMBER) 28

THURSDAY (SEPTEMBER) 29

FRIDAY (SEPTEMBER) 30

SATURDAY 1

◐ **SUNDAY** 2

October 2022

MONDAY
3

TUESDAY
YOM KIPPUR (BEGINS AT SUNDOWN)
4

WEDNESDAY
5

THURSDAY
6

FRIDAY

7

SATURDAY

8

SUNDAY

9

SUKKOT (BEGINS AT SUNDOWN)

Speak the Hunter Moon
affirmation while under the light
of the Full Moon: *I prioritize my
emotional safety and stability and
know how to care for myself and
my emotions at all times.*

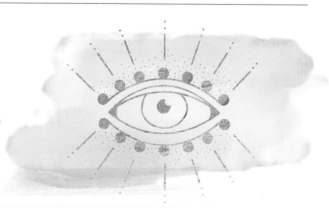

MONDAY

INDIGENOUS PEOPLES' DAY (US) /
COLUMBUS DAY (US)
THANKSGIVING DAY (CAN)

10

TUESDAY

11

WEDNESDAY

12

THURSDAY

13

FRIDAY

14

SATURDAY

15

SUNDAY

16

HUNTER MOON CRYSTAL

Smoky quartz is a gray and brown translucent stone that is known for its ability to keep you strongly grounded and protected. This crystal acts as a shield against emotional stress and is a wonderful stone to use for meditation. This form of quartz can assist your root chakra, which connects you to your foundation and stability. To connect with this stone, you can keep it in your pocket or wear it connected to your belt or a pant loop.

MONDAY
SIMCHAT TORAH (BEGINS AT SUNDOWN)

17

TUESDAY

18

WEDNESDAY

19

THURSDAY

20

FRIDAY   21

SATURDAY   22

SUNDAY   23

"There's nothing wrong with you . . .
Not even the darkest corner of that
beautiful soul."

—VICKI PETTERSSON

October 2022

MONDAY 24
LABOUR DAY (NZ)

◯ **TUESDAY** 25

WEDNESDAY 26

THURSDAY 27

FRIDAY

28

SATURDAY

29

SUNDAY

30

The best time to set up your emotional foundation is first thing in the morning. Prioritizing your emotional mindset will put you in a more present, clear, and stable state to tackle your day with intentionality.

November
Beaver Moon

Each November, the beavers retreat to their dams to make it through the long, hard winter. This is the source of this moon's name. The beavers' well-crafted sanctuaries create a space of safety for them during the coldest of days. This is a time to focus on your own physical sanctuary. You are being called to pour energy, effort, and attention into the conscious curation of your home to create a comfortable and beautiful environment in which you can relax, reset, and recharge.

FIRST QUARTER MOON RITUAL

This phase of the lunar cycle is about being decisive and taking action to manifest your intention. Much as it can be difficult to make a clear and organized decision when your mind feels cluttered and disorganized, it can be difficult to make a decision in a messy home. To keep your space tidy, you are going to create a master list for the maintenance of your sanctuary.

SANCTUARY MAINTENANCE LIST

What you need:
- Sheet of paper
- Colored pens
- Ruler

1. Lay out your paper and colored pens.

2. Using the ruler, draw a horizontal line across the middle of the paper. Your paper should be separated into a top half and a bottom half.

3. Now you will divide the bottom half. Using the ruler, draw a vertical line down the middle of the bottom half.

4. The top section is for things you do daily. The bottom left is things you do weekly. The bottom right is things you do monthly.

5. Fill out the sections. Here are some suggestions to get you started. Add anything else that is specific to your home.

DAILY:
- Make bed
- Wash dishes
- Take out trash

WEEKLY:
- Vacuum
- Wash clothes and sheets
- Clean bathrooms

MONTHLY:
- Organize, eliminate, and donate
- Wipe down baseboards
- Scrub showers

November 2022

NOTES	SUNDAY	MONDAY	TUESDAY
			1
			ALL SAINTS' DAY
	6	7	8
	DAYLIGHT SAVING TIME ENDS (US / CAN)		ELECTION DAY (US)
	13	14	15
	20	21	22
	27	28	29

November 2022

WEDNESDAY	THURSDAY	FRIDAY	SATURDAY
2	3	4	5
9	10	11 VETERANS DAY (US)	12
16	17	18	19
23	24 THANKSGIVING DAY (US)	25 NATIVE AMERICAN HERITAGE DAY (US)	26
30			

MONDAY (OCTOBER)
HALLOWEEN

31

TUESDAY
ALL SAINTS' DAY

1

WEDNESDAY

2

THURSDAY

3

FRIDAY

4

SATURDAY

5

SUNDAY
DAYLIGHT SAVING TIME ENDS (US / CAN)

6

November 2022

MONDAY
7

TUESDAY
ELECTION DAY (US)
8

WEDNESDAY
9

THURSDAY
10

FRIDAY
VETERANS DAY (US)

11

SATURDAY

12

SUNDAY

13

Speak the Beaver Moon affirmation while under the light of the Full Moon: *I live in a consciously curated space where I can relax, reset, and recharge. My home is my sanctuary.*

MONDAY 14

TUESDAY 15

WEDNESDAY 16

THURSDAY 17

FRIDAY

18

SATURDAY

19

SUNDAY

20

BEAVER MOON CRYSTAL

Black tourmaline is a striated, dark black stone that can be translucent
or opaque. This crystal is known as a powerful protector and a great
grounding stone. It can assist with protecting your home, ensuring that
negative energy is not allowed to enter. It can also give you a feeling of
being grounded and stable. To connect with this stone, you can display it
near the entryway of your home or wear it as a bracelet.

November 2022

MONDAY 21

TUESDAY 22

○ **WEDNESDAY** 23

THURSDAY 24
THANKSGIVING DAY (US)

FRIDAY
NATIVE AMERICAN HERITAGE DAY (US)

25

SATURDAY

26

SUNDAY

27

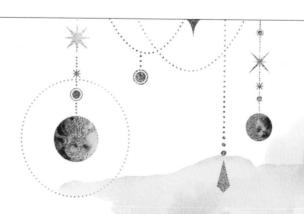

"Let your home be a sanctuary that gives you peace."
—AVINA CELESTE

December
Cold Moon

As winter takes center stage, December enters with her dark days and frigid temperatures. The extreme cold of the year's final month is the source of the name for this icy moon. This is a time to acknowledge the fire of your spirit. You are being called to identify what it is that lights you up from within and what it is that provides you with warmth. This moon is here to remind you to fan the flames of your passions.

WAXING GIBBOUS MOON RITUAL

This is a time for you to make any adjustments that are necessary to help your intentions manifest. To help with this concept, you will engage in a stretching exercise that demonstrates that even the smallest adjustments get you closer to your goal.

HOT MUSCLE STRETCHING EXERCISE

1. Go into your bathroom and take a hot shower with the bathroom door closed. Your muscles will be relaxed from the heat. Dry off, but remain unclothed in the steamy room.

2. Slowly bend down and reach toward your toes with your knees slightly flexed. Go as far as you can and hold the stretch for 20 seconds.

3. Roll yourself back up to a standing position. Breathe deeply.

4. Slowly bend down and reach toward your toes again. Go as far as you can and hold the stretch for 30 seconds.

5. Roll back up to a standing position and breathe.

6. When you are ready, bend over again and reach toward your toes. Feel your muscles stretch and lengthen. Go as far as you can and hold the stretch for 40 seconds.

7. Slowly roll back up and breathe.

8. You were likely able to get closer to your toes on the third attempt than you were on the first. Reflect on this: If I take the time to warm myself up and dedicate myself to continual small adjustments, I will get closer to my goal.

December 2022

NOTES	SUNDAY	MONDAY	TUESDAY
	4	5	6
	11	12	13
	18	19	20
	HANUKKAH (BEGINS AT SUNDOWN)		
	25	26	27
	CHRISTMAS DAY	BOXING DAY (UK / CAN / AUS / NZ) KWANZAA	

December 2022

WEDNESDAY	THURSDAY	FRIDAY	SATURDAY
	1 WORLD AIDS DAY	2	3 INTERNATIONAL DAY OF PERSONS WITH DISABILITIES
● 7	8	9	10 HUMAN RIGHTS DAY
14	15	☾ 16	17
21 WINTER SOLSTICE	22 ○	23	24 CHRISTMAS EVE
28 ☾	29	30	31 NEW YEAR'S EVE

MONDAY (NOVEMBER)   28

TUESDAY (NOVEMBER)   29

WEDNESDAY (NOVEMBER)   30

THURSDAY   1
WORLD AIDS DAY

FRIDAY   2

SATURDAY   3
INTERNATIONAL DAY OF PERSONS WITH DISABILITIES

SUNDAY   4

MONDAY 5

TUESDAY 6

● WEDNESDAY 7

THURSDAY 8

FRIDAY

9

SATURDAY
HUMAN RIGHTS DAY

10

SUNDAY

11

Speak the Cold Moon affirmation while under the light of the Full
Moon: *I light my own internal flame. My passions are the fuel for this
fire. Exhale. If you feel called, light a fire and warm yourself near it.*

December 2022

MONDAY 12

TUESDAY 13

WEDNESDAY 14

THURSDAY 15

FRIDAY

16

SATURDAY

17

SUNDAY
HANUKKAH (BEGINS AT SUNDOWN)

18

COLD MOON CRYSTAL

Fire agate is a brown stone that is full of sparkling
flame-like iridescence. This crystal helps increase
your passion and align you with your truest
desires. Are you in touch with what lights you up?
This crystal can help you enhance this connection.

MONDAY 19

TUESDAY 20

WEDNESDAY
WINTER SOLSTICE 21

THURSDAY 22

O **FRIDAY** 23

SATURDAY 24
CHRISTMAS EVE

SUNDAY 25
CHRISTMAS DAY

"The most powerful weapon on Earth is the human soul on fire."
—FERDINAND FOCH

January
Wolf Moon

January signifies fresh beginnings, but it is also a harsh time in the natural world: long nights, freezing terrain, and limited food sources. This moon was named after the wolves who would howl while in search of their next meal. Wolves are resilient and designed to survive—and even thrive—during the scarcest months of winter. The wolf bravely ventures off alone in search of sustenance because it trusts its innate instinct. *This is a time to acknowledge what you are hungry for in your life. Trust your intuition and reconnect with your wildness. You are called to forge your own path and to deeply trust your animal instinct.*

FULL MOON RITUAL

Bring elements of nature inside, light a candle to call on the wildness
of fire, or open a window to invite in the sounds of the evening.
If saying a blessing feels right for you, incorporate words of release:
freedom, space, openness, protection.

NOURISH YOUR BODY

Give yourself a soothing hand massage with hand cream.

SHIFT YOUR SPIRIT

Sit comfortably in your sacred space and meditate, breathing in and out
rhythmically, for 5 minutes.

Breathe deeply and answer the following prompts in your journal:

1. Am I connected to my animal instinct? Why or why not?

2. Are there elements of the wolf that I admire or fear that
   are becoming a part of me? Why or why not?

3. Is my greatest desire burning brightly? Why or why not?

4. Am I ready to share my greatest secret? Why or why not?
   After finishing these prompts, underline your
   "why not" responses.
   Go outdoors. Find a patch of earth that is lit by
   the moon. Dig a small hole here while connecting to
   your canine energy.

5. Take the paper you've written on and tear it into pieces.
   Drop these pieces into the hole and cover them with earth.

6. Take a cube of ice and place it on top of the covered hole.
   Breathe deeply as you watch the ice melt, and visualize all
   your obstacles melting with it.

7. When the ice has melted, exhale as a sign of release.

January 2023

NOTES	SUNDAY	MONDAY	TUESDAY
	1	2	3
	NEW YEAR'S DAY	BANK HOLIDAY (UK-SCT)	
	8	9	10
	15	16	17
		CIVIL RIGHTS DAY MARTIN LUTHER KING JR. DAY (US)	
	22	23	24
	CHINESE NEW YEAR		
	29	30	31

January 2023

WEDNESDAY	THURSDAY	FRIDAY	SATURDAY
4	5 ●	6	7
11	12	13	14 ★
18	19	20 ○	21
25	26	27	28
	AUSTRALIA DAY	HOLOCAUST REMEMBRANCE DAY	

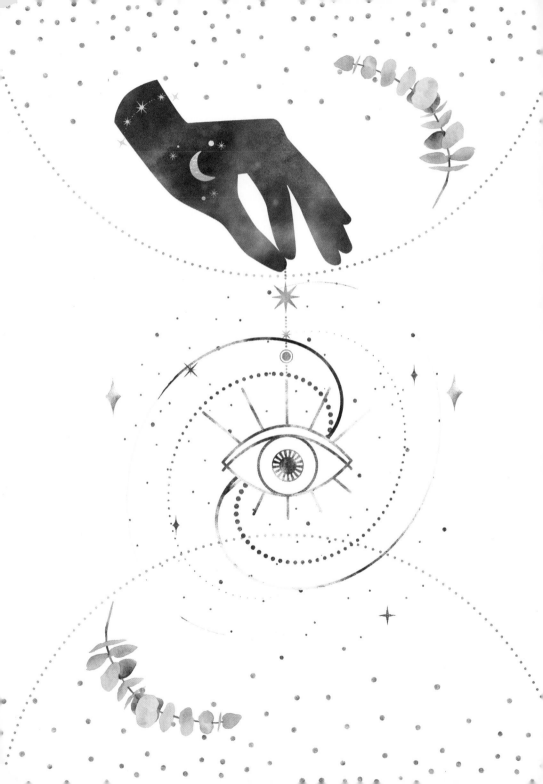

December / January 2023

MONDAY (DECEMBER)   26
BOXING DAY (UK / CAN / AUS / NZ) / KWANZAA

TUESDAY (DECEMBER)   27

WEDNESDAY (DECEMBER)   28

THURSDAY (DECEMBER)   29

FRIDAY (DECEMBER)   30

SATURDAY (DECEMBER)   31
NEW YEAR'S EVE

SUNDAY   1
NEW YEAR'S DAY

January 2023

MONDAY
BANK HOLIDAY (UK-SCT)

2

TUESDAY

3

WEDNESDAY

4

THURSDAY

5

FRIDAY

6

SATURDAY

7

SUNDAY

8

Speak this Wolf Moon affirmation while under the light of the Full Moon: *I am wild, free, and brave. My spirit came here with all the knowledge I need to thrive in this world. I live a courageous life and I inspire others to do the same.*

January 2023

MONDAY 9

TUESDAY 10

WEDNESDAY 11

THURSDAY 12

FRIDAY
13

SATURDAY
14

SUNDAY
15

WOLF MOON CRYSTAL
Labradorite is an iridescent stone believed to strengthen
your intuition, align you with your calling, and cut through
falsehoods. When thinking about fully communicating your
truth, visualize the wolf howling. This howl is a fully liberated
form of communication. You were born with a strong instinct
and intuition—do you listen to it?

January 2023

MONDAY
CIVIL RIGHTS DAY / MARTIN LUTHER KING JR. DAY (US)

16

TUESDAY

17

WEDNESDAY

18

THURSDAY

19

FRIDAY
20

○ SATURDAY
21

SUNDAY
CHINESE NEW YEAR
22

"Some days I am more
wolf than woman and I am
still learning how to stop
apologizing for my wild."
—NIKITA GILL

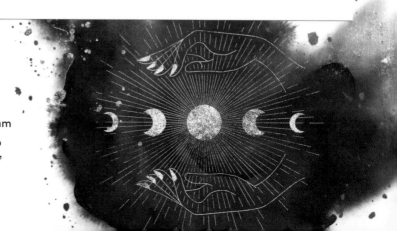

January 2023

MONDAY 23

TUESDAY 24

WEDNESDAY 25

THURSDAY 26
AUSTRALIA DAY

FRIDAY
HOLOCAUST REMEMBRANCE DAY

27

SATURDAY

28

SUNDAY

29

This is a time to practice gratitude. Gratitude is taking the time to acknowledge and receive the blessings in your life. Learning to acknowledge the good that exists, even if it is alongside the bad, is a positive mindset practice that can benefit your mood, outlook, and focus.

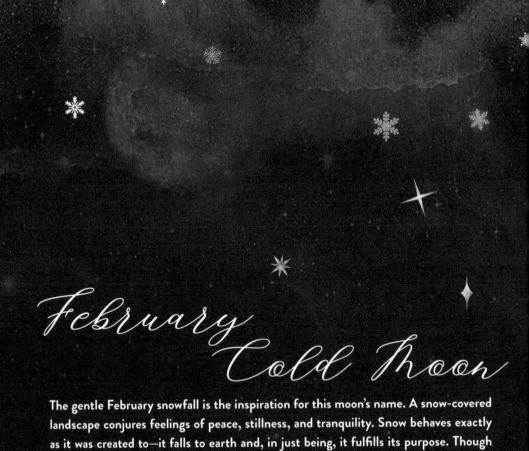

February
Cold Moon

The gentle February snowfall is the inspiration for this moon's name. A snow-covered landscape conjures feelings of peace, stillness, and tranquility. Snow behaves exactly as it was created to—it falls to earth and, in just being, it fulfills its purpose. Though the snow seems to make the world disappear, it is simply cloaking the earth beneath— hidden and waiting to reveal itself after the snow has melted. This is a time to immerse yourself in quiet reflection. Get to know yourself deeply, beneath the surface. Listen to your internal voice of knowing. You are being called to slow down and embrace your

NEW MOON RITUAL

This intention-setting ritual will focus on the themes of snow—stillness, peace, and the comfort of just being—to get you in alignment with this lunar cycle.

SET THE SPACE

To invoke stillness, you can blanket your area in white, covering a surface in a tablecloth or bedsheet, or you can dress in white. To invoke peace, light a lavender-scented candle. If saying a blessing before you begin, use words that the image of snow summons: still, pure, tranquil, white light.

SHIFT YOUR SPIRIT
BINAURAL BEATS + SNOW VISUALIZATION

To reach a place of stillness, you can listen to sounds of different frequencies in each ear. Your brain registers the frequency that is the difference between the two. This is called a binaural beat. Binaural beats mirror the mental state that occurs in meditation. You can find binaural beats online or downloaded.

1. Sitting in a comfortable, quiet space put your headphones on and play the binaural beat. Close your eyes and breathe slowly.

2. Begin this visualization:
   You are gazing over a beautiful landscape blanketed in white.
   Snow is gently falling. Let yourself relax deeply and enjoy the peace here. Imagine you are a snowflake. Visualize yourself high in the air, slowly drifting down to the earth. You trust that you know exactly how to fall gently to the ground. You know your purpose is just to be—to allow yourself to fall down from the sky. Feel yourself gently land on the snow-covered earth and exhale.

   Open your eyes.

February 2023

NOTES	SUNDAY	MONDAY	TUESDAY
	5	6	7
	WAITANGI DAY (NZ)	WAITANGI DAY OBSERVED (NZ)	
	12	13	14
			VALENTINE'S DAY
	19	20	21
		PRESIDENTS' DAY (US)	
	26	27	28

February 2023

WEDNESDAY	THURSDAY	FRIDAY	SATURDAY
1 **FIRST DAY OF BLACK HISTORY MONTH**	2 **GROUNDHOG DAY (US / CAN)**	3	4
8	9	10	11
15	16	17	18
22 **ASH WEDNESDAY**	23	24	25

January / February 2023

MONDAY (JANUARY)
30

TUESDAY (JANUARY)
31

WEDNESDAY
FIRST DAY OF BLACK HISTORY MONTH
1

THURSDAY
GROUNDHOG DAY (US / CAN)
2

FRIDAY
3

SATURDAY
4

SUNDAY
WAITANGI DAY (NZ)
5

February 2023

MONDAY
WAITANGI DAY OBSERVED (NZ)

6

TUESDAY

7

WEDNESDAY

8

THURSDAY

9

FRIDAY   10

SATURDAY   11

SUNDAY   12

Speak this Snow Moon affirmation
aloud: *I create my own peace and
tranquility. I enjoy spending time in
quiet communion with myself and
with my inner knowing. I trust and
allow my spirit to guide me. My being
is more than enough.*

February 2023

MONDAY   13

TUESDAY   14
VALENTINE'S DAY

WEDNESDAY   15

THURSDAY   16

FRIDAY 17

SATURDAY 18

SUNDAY 19

SNOW MOON CRYSTAL

Amethyst is a beautiful stone that comes in a variety of shades of purple. This crystal helps create an environment of calm, enhances mental clarity, and gets you in sync with your natural insights. Are you in touch with yourself—your intuition, spirituality, and deep inner knowing? This crystal can help you enhance this connection.

○ MONDAY
PRESIDENTS' DAY (US)

20

TUESDAY

21

WEDNESDAY
ASH WEDNESDAY

22

THURSDAY

23

FRIDAY

24

SATURDAY

25

SUNDAY

26

"I wonder if the snow loves the trees and fields, that it kisses them so gently?
And then it covers them up snug, you know, with a white quilt; and perhaps it says,
'Go to sleep, darlings, till the summer comes again.'"
—LEWIS CARROLL, *THROUGH THE LOOKING-GLASS*

March
Sap Moon

As March appears, the frost melts away. The warmth brings the sap within the trees to life and it begins to flow. This is how the Sap Moon got its name. The sap in the tree waits for the thaw. This is a metaphor for your life: you may be going through a difficult time, but there is an endless well of love within you—you just need to thaw out and tap into it. *This is a time to pay homage to yourself by cultivating self-love. You are being called to prioritize your self-care practices to tap into the self-love waiting inside you.*

WAXING GIBBOUS MOON RITUAL

This point in the lunar cycle is an ideal time to reflect on your actions and change course if that will help your intention manifest. To find a peaceful, stress-free environment in which to reflect, you don't have to travel far. With a few hotel-inspired tweaks to your space, you can take yourself on a mental getaway without leaving your home.

STAYCATION AT HOME

To make your space feel like a hotel, try the following:

- Take off all your makeup and wrap yourself in a plush robe and cozy slippers.
- Wash your bedsheets and make your bed. Pay special attention to crisp corners and smooth sheets.
- Add arrangements of fresh-cut flowers.
- Use a room spray or an essential oil to make the space smell elegant.
- Play light ambient music.
- Serve yourself lemon water out of a carafe and drink it out of a beautiful glass.
- Have a luxe cozy blanket nearby.
- Put some fancy chocolates in a serving dish.
- Upgrade your toiletries. Invest in quality body wash, shampoo, conditioner, and lotion. When your space is ready, block out a few uninterrupted hours. Turn off your phone and eat something decadent in your bathrobe—you can think of it as room service. When you feel yourself slip into your vacation mindset, reflect on what you could be doing differently to help your intention come true.

March 2023

NOTES	SUNDAY	MONDAY	TUESDAY
	5	6 ●	7
		PURIM (BEGINS AT SUNDOWN)	LABOUR DAY (AUS-ACT / NSW / SA)
	12	13	14
	DAYLIGHT SAVING TIME BEGINS (US / CAN)	LABOUR DAY (AUS-VIC)	
	19	20 ○	21
	MOTHERING SUNDAY (UK)	SPRING EQUINOX	NOWRUZ
	26	27 ◗	28

March 2023

WEDNESDAY	THURSDAY	FRIDAY	SATURDAY
1 **FIRST DAY OF WOMEN'S HISTORY MONTH**	2	3	4
8	9	10	11
15	16	17 **ST. PATRICK'S DAY**	18
22 **RAMADAN (BEGINS AT SUNDOWN)**	23	24	25
29	30	31	

February / March 2023

MONDAY (FEBRUARY) 27

TUESDAY (FEBRUARY) 28

WEDNESDAY 1
FIRST DAY OF WOMEN'S HISTORY MONTH

THURSDAY 2

FRIDAY 3

SATURDAY 4

SUNDAY 5

March 2023

MONDAY
PURIM (BEGINS AT SUNDOWN)

6

TUESDAY
LABOUR DAY (AUS-ACT / NSW / SA)

7

WEDNESDAY

8

THURSDAY

9

FRIDAY

10

SATURDAY

11

SUNDAY
DAYLIGHT SAVING TIME BEGINS (US / CAN)

12

Speak the Sap Moon
affirmation while under the light
of the Full Moon: *I love myself
unconditionally. I prioritize my
needs and my self-care practice
to consistently show myself the
love that I know I am worthy of.*

MONDAY
LABOUR DAY (AUS-VIC)

13

TUESDAY

14

◗ WEDNESDAY

15

THURSDAY

16

FRIDAY
ST. PATRICK'S DAY

17

SATURDAY

18

SUNDAY
MOTHERING SUNDAY (UK)

19

SAP MOON CRYSTAL

Rose quartz is a light pink stone with a subtle sparkle. This crystal is used to enhance love of all kinds and can be specifically helpful when used in your self-love practice. Do you struggle with accepting and loving yourself completely? This stone can help facilitate an understanding of unconditional love and help you learn to love yourself in this way.

March 2023

MONDAY
SPRING EQUINOX

20

○ **TUESDAY**
NOWRUZ

21

WEDNESDAY
RAMADAN (BEGINS AT SUNDOWN)

22

THURSDAY

23

FRIDAY   24

SATURDAY   25

SUNDAY   26

"When a woman becomes her
own best friend, life is easier."
—DIANE VON FURSTENBERG

April
Pink Moon

The vibrant pink of the first blooms of April gives this moon its name. Just as these blooms use their beauty to signal warmer and easier seasons, your spirit is being called to emerge from its hibernation to create warmer and easier times for others. This lunar cycle is a time for your spirit, heart, and energy to shine vibrantly. You are being called to courageously show up as your authentic self. It is time for you to identify and share your unique soul gifts with the world.

FIRST QUARTER MOON RITUAL

It is common to be stuck in the past—which shows up as feelings like guilt and regret—or fixated on the future—which can feel like anxiety or fear. When your mind is occupied with these thoughts, you are missing out on the experience you could be having in the moment—what's happening to you right now. It is only by developing your awareness of the now that you will be able to make the correct decisions and take the appropriate actions to further your intentions, become aware of your soul gifts, and know when and where it is appropriate to use these gifts. This exercise will ground you in your body and slow down your mind so that you can be fully present in this moment.

USING YOUR SENSES TO BECOME PRESENT

1. Find a comfortable place to sit.

2. Breathe deeply in and out with your eyes open until you begin to relax.

3. Review all your senses, one at a time. Ask yourself:
    - What do I see at the present moment?
    - What do I hear at the present moment?
    - What do I smell at the present moment?
    - What do I taste at the present moment?
    - What do I feel at the present moment?

4. Answer these questions in your mind one at a time until you fully acknowledge your surroundings and present experience. You are now aware of your present moment.

5. Feel free to repeat this exercise anytime you want to be fully present.

April 2023

NOTES	SUNDAY	MONDAY	TUESDAY
	2 PALM SUNDAY	3	4
	9 EASTER	10	11
	16 ORTHODOX EASTER	17 YOM HASHOAH (BEGINS AT SUNDOWN)	18
	23 / 30	24	25 ANZAC DAY (AUS / NZ)

April 2023

WEDNESDAY	THURSDAY	FRIDAY	SATURDAY
			1 **APRIL FOOLS' DAY**
5 **PASSOVER (BEGINS AT SUNDOWN)**	● 6	7 **GOOD FRIDAY**	8
12	☽ 13	14	15
19	○ 20	21 **EID AL-FITR (BEGINS AT SUNDOWN)**	22 **EARTH DAY**
26 **ADMINISTRATIVE PROFESSIONALS' DAY (US)**	☾ 27	28	29

March / April 2023

MONDAY (MARCH)   27

TUESDAY (MARCH)   28

WEDNESDAY (MARCH)   29

THURSDAY (MARCH)   30

FRIDAY (MARCH)   31

SATURDAY
APRIL FOOLS' DAY   1

SUNDAY
PALM SUNDAY   2

April 2023

MONDAY 3

TUESDAY 4

WEDNESDAY 5
PASSOVER (BEGINS AT SUNDOWN)

● **THURSDAY** 6

FRIDAY
GOOD FRIDAY

7

SATURDAY

8

SUNDAY
EASTER

9

Speak the Pink Moon affirmation
while under the light of the Full
Moon: *I acknowledge and give energy
to my unique gifts that I lovingly and
openly share with the world.*

April 2023

MONDAY 10

TUESDAY 11

WEDNESDAY 12

◗ **THURSDAY** 13

FRIDAY

14

SATURDAY

15

SUNDAY
ORTHODOX EASTER

16

PINK MOON CRYSTAL

Quartz crystal is a colorless or white gemstone that is known as the "master healer." This crystal helps keep you connected to your spiritual gifts and wisdom. Are you in touch with your inherent gifts and do you share them with others? This crystal can help you enhance this connection.

MONDAY
YOM HASHOAH (BEGINS AT SUNDOWN)

17

TUESDAY

18

WEDNESDAY

19

○ THURSDAY

20

FRIDAY
EID AL-FITR (BEGINS AT SUNDOWN)

21

SATURDAY
EARTH DAY

22

SUNDAY

23

"I saw it written and I saw it say
Pink Moon is on its way."
—NICK DRAKE

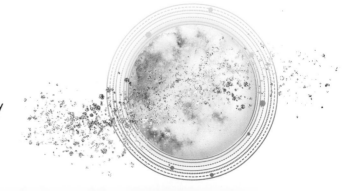

MONDAY

24

TUESDAY
ANZAC DAY (AUS / NZ)

25

WEDNESDAY
ADMINISTRATIVE PROFESSIONALS' DAY (US)

26

◖ THURSDAY

27

FRIDAY 28

SATURDAY 29

SUNDAY 30

As the Pink Moon is tied to giving back and sharing, this is a perfect time to share your soul gifts—the natural talents, abilities, passions, and strengths—you have cultivated.

May
Flower Moon

May brings warmer weather and, with it, an array of blooming flowers. This gorgeous display by Mother Nature gave this moon its name. The Flower Moon is tied to the floral themes of abundant beauty and flowering fertility. These concepts are tied to feminine energy, as are all things related to creation. Feminine energy is not exclusive to those who identify as female, but is part of the energy that each soul possesses. This lunar cycle is a time to acknowledge and honor the strength of your roots. You are being called to allow yourself to fully bloom and to connect to your divine feminine energy.

WAXING CRESCENT MOON RITUAL

This is the ideal time in the lunar cycle to plant seeds for future growth, both literally and figuratively. You are figuratively planting seeds when you direct energy toward your intention. You will be literally planting seeds for future growth in this next exercise.

FLOWERING WINDOWSILL

What you need:

- Peat moss
- Egg carton
- Spray bottle filled with water
- African violet seeds
- Plastic wrap
- Pot or container with drainage holes
- Indoor potting soil

1. Place peat moss in the egg carton, filling each section to the top.

2. Fully dampen all the peat moss with your spray bottle.

3. Place a couple seeds in each section of the carton on top of the peat moss. Lightly mist the seeds with the spray bottle.

4. Cover the carton loosely with plastic wrap. Place it on a windowsill that receives indirect sunlight.

5. Check your seedlings every few days, removing the plastic wrap and misting with water if you notice the peat moss drying out. Replace the plastic wrap after each misting.

6. In 1 to 9 weeks, your seeds should germinate.

7. When the seedling has a leaf $\frac{1}{2}$ inch wide, it is ready to be transplanted.

8. Fill your pot with indoor potting soil. Gently remove your seedling with roots intact from the carton, make a hole in the potting soil and plant it in the pot, gently firming the soil around the root.

9. Keep this pot on a windowsill and mist your flowers when you notice the soil drying out. This technique can provide you with an indoor garden that flowers year-round and reminds you that taking the time to plant and care for seeds eventually leads to something beautiful blooming.

May 2023

NOTES	SUNDAY	MONDAY	TUESDAY
		1 **LABOUR DAY (AUS-QLD)** **EARLY MAY BANK HOLIDAY (UK)** **FIRST DAY OF ASIAN AMERICAN AND PACIFIC ISLANDER HERITAGE MONTH**	2
	7	8	9
	14 **MOTHER'S DAY (US / CAN)**	15	16
	21	22 **VICTORIA DAY (CAN)**	23
	28	29 **SPRING BANK HOLIDAY (UK)** **MEMORIAL DAY (US)**	30

May 2023

WEDNESDAY	THURSDAY	FRIDAY	SATURDAY
3	4	5	6
		CINCO DE MAYO	
10	11	12	13
17	18	19	20
24	25	26	27
31			

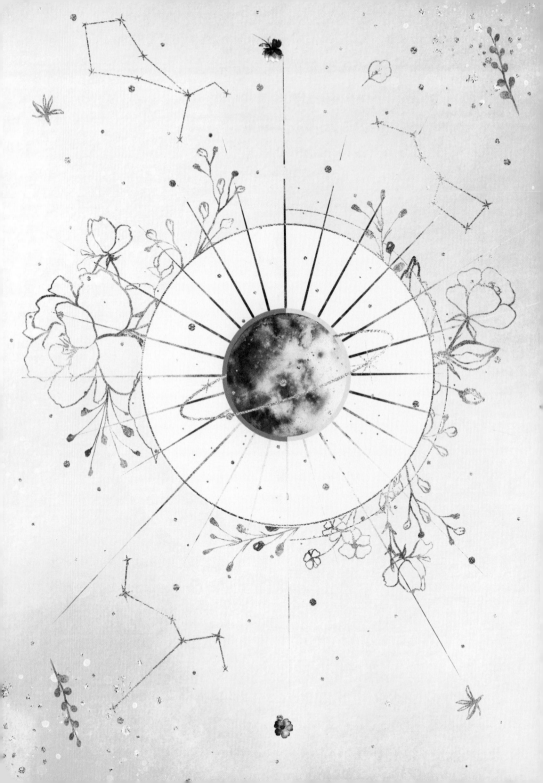

MONDAY

FIRST DAY OF ASIAN AMERICAN AND PACIFIC ISLANDER HERITAGE MONTH /
EARLY MAY BANK HOLIDAY UK /
LABOUR DAY (AUS-QLD)

1

TUESDAY

2

WEDNESDAY

3

THURSDAY

4

FRIDAY

CINCO DE MAYO

5

SATURDAY

6

SUNDAY

7

May 2023

MONDAY 8

TUESDAY 9

WEDNESDAY 10

THURSDAY 11

FRIDAY

12

SATURDAY

13

SUNDAY
MOTHER'S DAY (US / CAN)

14

Speak the Flower Moon affirmation
while under the light of the Full Moon:
*I am beautiful, perfectly made, and
divinely feminine. I love and nurture my
femininity and trust that it leads me to
the places where I fully bloom.*

May 2023

MONDAY 15

TUESDAY 16

WEDNESDAY 17

THURSDAY 18

○ FRIDAY

19

SATURDAY

20

SUNDAY

21

FLOWER MOON CRYSTAL

Carnelian is an orange gemstone that is thought to
encourage emotional warmth and improve fertility,
both concepts connected with divine feminine energy.
This crystal helps eradicate emotional negativity and
awaken your feminine creativity. Are you in touch with
your feminine side? This crystal can help you enhance
this connection.

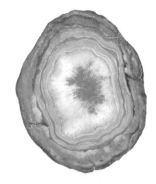

May 2023

MONDAY VICTORIA DAY (CAN)   22

TUESDAY   23

WEDNESDAY   24

THURSDAY   25

FRIDAY   26

SATURDAY   27

SUNDAY   28

"I am in awe of flowers.
Not because of their
colors, but because even
though they have dirt
in their roots, they still
grow. They still bloom."
—D. ANTOINETTE FOY

June
Strawberry Moon

The arrival of strawberries is a clear sign of the arrival of summer. This is how this June moon received her name. Days of sunshine and sweetness are just beginning—this is no time to think about the harsh winter that now seems to be in the distant past. This lunar cycle is a time to reflect on the abundant sweetness in your life. You are being called to harvest the things you have carefully tended. You should avoid reviewing the past and instead look toward the future to experience gratitude for the present moment.

FULL MOON RITUAL
SET THE SPACE
Incorporate elements of abundance in your space by displaying photos of people you love or precious possessions. If you want to say a blessing, use words of release: clarity, perspective, exhale, let go.

SHIFT YOUR SPIRIT
If you have a scarcity mindset, it can be difficult to let go of things. This next exercise will shift your mindset to a place of abundance so you can release your illusion of scarcity.

TWO PILES ABUNDANCE EXERCISE
1. Take all of your clothing and place it on an open surface.
2. One item at a time, ask yourself: Do I love this item? If you do, place it in a pile to the left.
3. If you don't, ask yourself: Do I need this item? If you do, place it in the pile to the left. If you do not, place it in a pile to the right.
4. Do this for each item of clothing.
5. When you are done sorting, put away the items in the pile to the left.

RELEASE WHAT NO LONGER SERVES YOU
You are left with a pile of clothing that you do not love or need. You may have been under the illusion that you needed more clothing. The reality is that if there is even a single item in the pile in front of you, that means that you possess an abundance of clothing. It is time to release these remaining items and your scarcity mentality.

PAY IT FORWARD ABUNDANCE EXERCISE
1. For each item, ask yourself: Would someone I know enjoy this? If the answer is yes, put it in a gifting pile to the far left.
2. If the answer is no, ask yourself: Would someone I do not know enjoy this? If the answer is yes, put it in a donation pile in the middle.
3. If the answer is no, put it in a textile recycling pile to the far right.
4. Take the donation pile to a local store that accepts clothing donations.
5. Take the recycling pile to a local textile recycling location so the clothing can be responsibly upcycled.
6. Gift the items in your gift pile to the people you identified. In recognizing your abundance, recognize that you were able to grant your excess to others to fulfill their wants and needs.

June 2023

NOTES	SUNDAY	MONDAY	TUESDAY
	4	5	6
	11	12	13
	18	19	20
	FATHER'S DAY (US / CAN / UK)	JUNETEENTH (US)	
	25	26	27

June 2023

WEDNESDAY	THURSDAY	FRIDAY	SATURDAY
	1	2	3
	FIRST DAY OF PRIDE MONTH		
7	8	9	10
14	15	16	17
FLAG DAY (US)			
21	22	23	24
SUMMER SOLSTICE			
28	29	30	

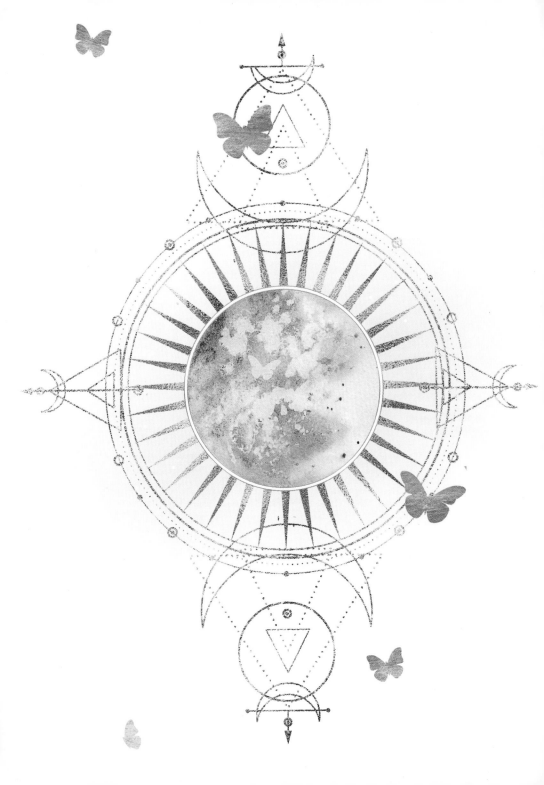

May / June 2023

MONDAY (MAY)
SPRING BANK HOLIDAY (UK) /
MEMORIAL DAY (US)

29

TUESDAY (MAY)

30

WEDNESDAY (MAY)

31

THURSDAY
FIRST DAY OF PRIDE MONTH

1

FRIDAY

2

● SATURDAY

3

SUNDAY

4

June 2023

MONDAY   5

TUESDAY   6

WEDNESDAY   7

THURSDAY   8

FRIDAY

9

SATURDAY

10

SUNDAY

11

Speak the Strawberry Moon affirmation
while under the light of the Full Moon:
*I have and will always have more than
I need. I am grateful for the sweet
abundance that is in my life.*

June 2023

MONDAY 12

TUESDAY 13

WEDNESDAY
FLAG DAY (US) 14

THURSDAY 15

FRIDAY

16

SATURDAY

17

○ SUNDAY
FATHER'S DAY (US / CAN / UK)S

18

STRAWBERRY MOON CRYSTAL

Hiddenite is a stone that comes in varying shades of green. This stone is tied with love and spontaneity, which helps keep you connected to the present moment. This crystal also assists with keeping gratitude in your life, and can open your heart chakra, which connects you to your emotional awareness of your life and the present moment. Are you in touch with a feeling of joyful abundance for where you are right now?

June 2023

MONDAY
JUNETEENTH HOLIDAY

19

TUESDAY

20

WEDNESDAY
SUMMER SOLSTICE

21

THURSDAY

22

FRIDAY 23

SATURDAY 24

SUNDAY 25

"But don't forget, in the
meantime, that this is the
season for strawberries."
—CLARICE LISPECTOR

July
Buck Moon

In synchronicity with the hot July sun, young bucks begin to sprout their antlers. This is a sign of the buck's impending independence. The antlers are an indication that the animal is ready to separate from the group and take control of his own life. This is a time for growth and maturation—a time to claim your independence. You are called to recognize the freedom and authority you have in your life and to acknowledge the wisdom that you possess to confidently make your own decisions.

NEW MOON RITUAL

This intention-setting ritual will focus on themes of maturity—independence, freedom, and wisdom—to get you in alignment with this lunar cycle. Forging a mind, body, and heart connection is a sign of growth and maturity.

SET THE SPACE

To invoke maturity and independence, put out photos of yourself as a child, nature, or a young buck. Place a stack of books on a surface to represent wisdom and tie them together with a string as a nod to your ability to set boundaries. If you are saying a blessing before you begin, use words that summon the concept of mature strength: self-assured, wise, capable, decisive.

NOURISH YOUR BODY

Eat a handful of trail mix—nuts and berries are loved by bucks.

FIRST POSITION:

Sit on the floor with your legs straight in front of you. With your arms outstretched, slowly and gently reach for your toes. Breathe in and out deeply. Think deep within your heart: I am strong and wise. Then say aloud, "I am strong and wise."

SECOND POSITION:

Stand with your feet shoulder width apart. Bend, then slowly and gently reach for your toes. Breathe in and out deeply. Think deep within your heart: I am free and maintain clear boundaries. Then say it aloud.

THIRD POSITION:

Stand with your feet shoulder width apart. Rise up onto your toes and reach as far as you can up toward the sky. Breathe in and out deeply. Think, deep within your heart: I am mature and take responsibility for my own life. Then say it aloud.

July 2023

NOTES	SUNDAY	MONDAY	TUESDAY
	2	● 3	4
			INDEPENDENCE DAY (US)
	◗ 9	10	11
	16	○ 17	18
	23	24	◖ 25
	30	31	

July 2023

WEDNESDAY	THURSDAY	FRIDAY	SATURDAY
			1 CANADA DAY (CAN)
5	6	7	8
12	13	14	15
19	20	21	22
26	27	28	29

MONDAY (JUNE) 26

TUESDAY (JUNE) 27

WEDNESDAY (JUNE) 28

THURSDAY (JUNE) 29

FRIDAY (JUNE) 30

SATURDAY
CANADA DAY (CAN)
1

SUNDAY 2

July 2023

MONDAY

3

TUESDAY
INDEPENDENCE DAY (US)

4

WEDNESDAY

5

THURSDAY

6

FRIDAY

7

SATURDAY

8

◗ SUNDAY

9

Speak the Buck Moon affirmation while under
the light of the Full Moon: *I am strong and
capable and I make the decisions in my life.*

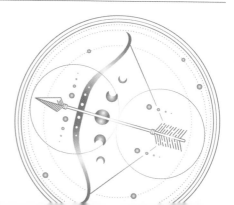

July 2023

MONDAY 10

TUESDAY 11

WEDNESDAY 12

THURSDAY 13

FRIDAY
14

SATURDAY
15

SUNDAY
16

BUCK MOON CRYSTAL

Yellow jasper is a vibrant stone that is known to enhance the feeling of being complete. This crystal helps connect you to your innate wisdom and establish clear boundaries. It is thought to be a protective stone that absorbs negative energy. Are you in touch with your own freedom? This crystal can assist with this connection.

O **MONDAY**   17

TUESDAY   18

WEDNESDAY   19

THURSDAY   20

FRIDAY
21

SATURDAY
22

SUNDAY
23

"Every great dream begins with a
dreamer. Always remember, you
have within you the strength, the
patience, and the passion to reach
for the stars to change the world."
—HARRIET TUBMAN

July 2023

MONDAY 24

◖ **TUESDAY** 25

WEDNESDAY 26

THURSDAY 27

FRIDAY 28

SATURDAY 29

SUNDAY 30

As the Buck Moon is about independence and autonomy, you likely owe *yourself* some gratitude. Affirm yourself by saying aloud: *Thank you, Self, for investing time and energy in my physical, emotional, and spiritual well-being.*

August
Sturgeon Moon

The sturgeon that fill the Great Lakes in August of each year are the source of this moon's name. Even with an abundance of fish, patience and faith are still necessary virtues to successfully catch a fish—because one must wait for a fish to bite the line. As fish were a powerful form of currency in the past, you can apply the aforementioned concepts of abundance, patience, and faith to today's currency: money. This is a time to be thankful for the financial abundance and opportunities in your life. You are also being called to exercise careful planning, patience, and faith for the financial abundance to come.

WAXING CRESCENT MOON RITUAL

This phase of the lunar cycle is calling you to develop the intention you set. One way to aid your intention's development is by keeping energy focused on your objective. To keep yourself focused, you need to be accountable. Accountability means that you keep promises you make to yourself and others. The following exercise focuses on accountability.

MONEY TREE

What you need:
- Money tree plant in a pot
- Sheet of paper and pen

1. Find a location for your money tree plant. Consider two things: the plant's needs and guidance from feng shui. The tree craves bright indirect light and consistent temperature. Feng shui— the Chinese tradition of arranging items in your living space to promote good fortune—suggests that you place the tree in the back left section of your home, the area associated with money and abundance. Take these things into consideration and choose the perfect spot for your money tree.

2. Visit your tree daily. Water thoroughly when you notice the top level of the soil drying out.

3. During your daily visit, write a financial promise to yourself on the sheet of paper. Example: I will save $5 a day, or I will open a savings account by the end of the month.

4. At the end of the lunar cycle, take this list of financial abundance promises and fold it up. Place it in your wallet for safekeeping, as a constant reminder and a source of positive energy.

August 2023

NOTES	SUNDAY	MONDAY	TUESDAY
_____			1
_____	6	7	8
_____	13	14	15
_____	20	21	22
_____	27	28 **SUMMER BANK HOLIDAY (UK-ENG / NIR / WAL)**	29

August 2023

WEDNESDAY	THURSDAY	FRIDAY	SATURDAY
2	3	4	5
9	10	11	12
○ 16	17	18	19
23	◑ 24	25	26
● 30	31		

July / August 2023

MONDAY (JULY)	31
● **TUESDAY**	1
WEDNESDAY	2
THURSDAY	3
FRIDAY	4
SATURDAY	5
SUNDAY	6

August 2023

MONDAY 7

TUESDAY 8

WEDNESDAY 9

THURSDAY 10

FRIDAY   11

SATURDAY   12

SUNDAY   13

Speak this intention under the light of the Full
Moon: *Money flows to me easily and effortlessly
and I am grateful for this blessing.*

MONDAY 14

TUESDAY 15

○ **WEDNESDAY** 16

THURSDAY 17

FRIDAY

18

SATURDAY

19

SUNDAY

20

STURGEON MOON CRYSTAL

This deep, earthy red stone is known for its
motivational properties. This crystal helps attract
wealth, abundance, and energy. Are you in touch
with these elements of yourself? This gemstone
can help you enhance this connection.

August 2023

MONDAY 21

TUESDAY 22

WEDNESDAY 23

◖ **THURSDAY** 24

FRIDAY

25

SATURDAY

26

SUNDAY

27

"Great fish do not swim in shallow waters."
—MATSHONA DHLIWAYO

September Corn Moon

This September moon honors the harvesting of maize, a staple crop in Native American diets. This is a time to recognize the "staples" in your life and give gratitude for what is truly important and necessary to your existence. This is a time for you to acknowledge the staples in your life and to identify the things, habits, and people you deem foundational and necessary. *This is also a time to solidify all five necessary elements— physical, mental, emotional, spiritual, and social—of your self-care practice.*

THIRD QUARTER MOON RITUAL

This phase of the cycle is about letting go and cleansing. Though this is often focused on an emotional component, you will be focusing on a physical component this time: your clothing. Clothing is in contact with your skin each day. If it is uncomfortable, it can create a subtle strain on you throughout the day. Your goal is to become aware of the feeling of your clothing and to let go of any clothing that is not utterly comfortable.

COMFORTABLE CLOTHING FOR A WEEK

For seven days in a row, focus on the comfort of your clothing. You may not wear an outfit that is not completely comfortable from head to toe. This applies to all outfits you wear, including what you wear around the house and to sleep in.

To determine whether an item is comfortable, ask yourself the following questions after you put it on:

- Does it fit without tugging or pulling?
- Does the fabric feel good against my skin?
- Can I move comfortably in this?
- Do all buttons, hooks, and zippers close?

If you can answer in the affirmative to all the above questions, the garment can be worn. If not, fold it and place it in a pile. At the end of the seven days, the folded pile of clothing can be donated or gifted. State: *I let go of anything that makes me feel uncomfortable in my own skin. I am cleansed of this.*

September 2023

NOTES	SUNDAY	MONDAY	TUESDAY
	3	4	5
	FATHER'S DAY (AUS / NZ)	LABOR DAY (US) LABOUR DAY (CAN)	
	10	11	12
	GRANDPARENTS' DAY (US)	PATRIOT DAY (US)	
	17	18	19
	24	25	26
	YOM KIPPUR (BEGINS AT SUNDOWN)		

September 2023

WEDNESDAY	THURSDAY	FRIDAY	SATURDAY
		1	2
6	7	8	9
13	14	15 **ROSH HASHANAH (BEGINS AT SUNDOWN)** **FIRST DAY OF NATIONAL HISPANIC HERITAGE MONTH**	16
20	21	22	23 **FALL EQUINOX**
27	28	29 **SUKKOT (BEGINS AT SUNDOWN)**	30

MONDAY (AUGUST)
SUMMER BANK HOLIDAY (UK-ENG / NIR / WAL)

28

TUESDAY (AUGUST)

29

● **WEDNESDAY (AUGUST)**

30

THURSDAY (AUGUST)

31

FRIDAY

1

SATURDAY

2

SUNDAY
FATHER'S DAY (AUS / NZ)

3

September 2023

MONDAY
LABOR DAY (US) / LABOUR DAY (CAN)

4

TUESDAY

5

WEDNESDAY

6

THURSDAY

7

FRIDAY

8

SATURDAY

9

SUNDAY
GRANDPARENTS' DAY (US)

10

Set a routine doing something specific to care for yourself each day. Under the light of the moon, state the intention: *I prioritize my self-care and have a well-designed routine that I do daily.*

September 2023

MONDAY 11
PATRIOT DAY (US)

TUESDAY 12

WEDNESDAY 13

○ **THURSDAY** 14

FRIDAY

ROSH HASHANAH (BEGINS AT SUNDOWN) /
FIRST DAY OF NATIONAL HISPANIC HERITAGE MONTH

15

SATURDAY

16

SUNDAY

17

Being emotionally balanced is easier said than done. There are countless things swirling in your emotional subconscious that you may have pushed down or ignored to keep up with the fast pace of the world around you. These unchecked emotions can pile up and actually slow you down. That's why creating a habit of emotionally checking in with yourself is so important.

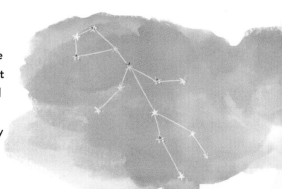

September 2023

MONDAY 18

TUESDAY 19

WEDNESDAY 20

THURSDAY 21

FRIDAY

22

SATURDAY
FALL EQUINOX

23

SUNDAY
YOM KIPPUR (BEGINS AT SUNDOWN)

24

"The day of fortune is like a
harvest day, We must be busy
when the corn is ripe."
—TORQUATO TASSO

October
Hunter Moon

The chilly October hunt to stock up for the long winter is the source of this moon's name. This is an encouragement to strategically prepare for your future and to know that you have what it takes to make it through difficult times. During this moon, prioritize incorporating emotional self-care into your daily life. Emotional self-care is a powerful foundation for a successful life.

FIRST QUARTER MOON RITUAL

As your intention is focused on something associated with your emotional wellness, the following activity helps you take specific action to tap into your emotional state more deeply. A haiku is a three-line poem with 5, 7, and 5 syllables in each line. Putting your emotions into writing helps make them tangible, accessible, and easier to deal with.

EMOTIONAL AWARENESS HAIKU EXERCISE

What you need:

1. Piece of paper and pen
2. Identify three emotions that you would like to handle more successfully.
3. Craft a haiku for each emotion, breaking down your emotional experience into three lines and a total of 17 syllables. You may need to try different combinations to make the words fit. Each time you restructure your thoughts, you revisit your emotional experience.

HERE ARE A COUPLE OF EXAMPLES TO ASSIST YOU:

If the emotion you chose was anger, you might write:

Swirling fit of rage
You consume my every thought
Why do you haunt me?

If the emotion you chose was anxiety, you might write:

My mind is racing
Again I won't sleep tonight
Waiting for the sun

Repeat this exercise anytime you are experiencing a strong emotion. Putting something that feels so big into 17 tiny syllables makes it feel more manageable.

October 2023

NOTES	SUNDAY	MONDAY	TUESDAY
	1	2	3
		LABOUR DAY (AUS-ACT / NSW / SA)	
	8	9	10
		INDIGENOUS PEOPLES' DAY (US) **COLUMBUS DAY (US)** **THANKSGIVING DAY (CAN)**	
	15	16	17
	22	23	24
		LABOUR DAY (NZ)	
	29	30	31
			HALLOWEEN

October 2023

WEDNESDAY	THURSDAY	FRIDAY	SATURDAY
4	5	6	7
			SIMCHAT TORAH (BEGINS AT SUNDOWN)
11	12	13	14
18	19	20	21
25	26	27	28

September / October 2023

MONDAY (SEPTEMBER) 25

TUESDAY (SEPTEMBER) 26

WEDNESDAY (SEPTEMBER) 27

THURSDAY (SEPTEMBER) 28

● **FRIDAY (SEPTEMBER)** 29
SUKKOT (BEGINS AT SUNDOWN)

SATURDAY (SEPTEMBER) 30

SUNDAY 1

October 2023

MONDAY 2
LABOUR DAY (AUS-ACT / NSW / SA)

TUESDAY 3

WEDNESDAY 4

THURSDAY 5

FRIDAY

6

SATURDAY

SIMCHAT TORAH (BEGINS AT SUNDOWN)

7

SUNDAY

8

Gaining clarity can be difficult, especially if you are experiencing emotions. To facilitate clarity, you can create a safe space where the overwhelm caused by emotions does not exist. If you are thinking, "This place doesn't exist"—you're right. You are the only one who can call this space into existence.

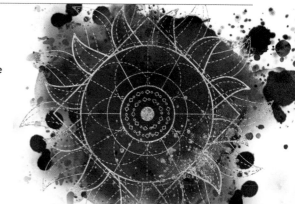

October 2023

MONDAY
**INDIGENOUS PEOPLES' DAY (US) /
COLUMBUS DAY (US) /
THANKSGIVING DAY (CAN)**

9

TUESDAY

10

WEDNESDAY

11

THURSDAY

12

FRIDAY 13

O **SATURDAY** 14

SUNDAY 15

When using creativity in your emotional self-care practice, remember that you are not being judged on the outcome. Creativity is all about the *process*, because this is where the emotional release occurs.

October 2023

MONDAY 16

TUESDAY 17

WEDNESDAY 18

THURSDAY 19

FRIDAY

20

SATURDAY

21

SUNDAY

22

"Many solemn nights
Blond moon, we stand and marvel . . .
Sleeping our noons away."
—TEITOKU, JAPANESE HAIKU

October 2023

MONDAY 23
LABOUR DAY (NZ)

TUESDAY 24

WEDNESDAY 25

THURSDAY 26

FRIDAY

27

● SATURDAY

28

SUNDAY

29

During this Hunter Moon, if you feel your
emotions are on shaky ground, say aloud:
*My emotional coping strategies are
clearly defined to carry me through
emotional challenges.*

November
Beaver Moon

Native Americans and early European settlers trapped beavers in November before the waters froze over and the beavers retreated to their dams. This is a time to prepare your "dam." This moon encourages you to make your home a sanctuary to keep you warm through dark and cold times.

NEW MOON RITUAL

This intention-setting ritual will focus on the themes of the
Beaver Moon—comfort, sanctuary, and home—to get you
in alignment with this lunar cycle.

SET THE SPACE

Incorporate elements of beauty, comfort, and safety into your space.
Choose items that bring you comfort and peace. If you are using black
tourmaline, place it somewhere visible and decorative. If saying a blessing
before you begin, use words that summon the image of home: peace, safety,
regeneration, cocoon.

NOURISH YOUR BODY

Sip a warm cup of lemon water with a pinch of
sea salt to balance and ground your being.

COZY AND SAFE CORNER CREATION

Identify an area of your home or space that you like. You are
creating a space that is all your own where you can feel protected
from any negative external influence. This is your sanctuary.
To craft this environment, you can include any of the following
elements or anything that makes you feel protected.

BLANKETS: Use a variety of plush and
soft textiles so you can wrap yourself up.

FRAMED ART AND PHOTOS:
Display images of visual interest that
soothe and inspire you.

BOOKS: Pick texts that are dreamy
and allow you to escape to another world.

ESSENTIAL OILS AND DIFFUSER:
Any oil you find calming or lovely can be
used to scent the space.

CANDLES: The flame is hypnotic and meditative.
You can also invest in an elegant candle snuffer.

MUSIC: Add a speaker or record
player to play your favorite tunes.

November 2023

NOTES	SUNDAY	MONDAY	TUESDAY
	◐ 5 **DAYLIGHT SAVING TIME ENDS (US / CAN)**	6	7 **ELECTION DAY (US)**
	12	○ 13	14
	19	◐ 20	21
	26	● 27	28

November 2023

WEDNESDAY	THURSDAY	FRIDAY	SATURDAY
1 ALL SAINTS' DAY	2	3	4
8	9	10	11 VETERANS DAY (US)
15	16	17	18
22	23 THANKSGIVING DAY (US)	24 NATIVE AMERICAN HERITAGE DAY (US)	25
29	30		

MONDAY (OCTOBER)

30

TUESDAY (OCTOBER)

HALLOWEEN

31

WEDNESDAY

ALL SAINTS' DAY

1

THURSDAY

2

FRIDAY

3

SATURDAY

4

SUNDAY

DAYLIGHT SAVING TIME ENDS (US / CAN)

5

November 2023

MONDAY   6

TUESDAY   7
ELECTION DAY (US)

WEDNESDAY   8

THURSDAY   9

FRIDAY

10

SATURDAY
VETERANS DAY (US)

11

SUNDAY

12

Under the light of the moon, say aloud,
*My home is a safe place of renewal and
regeneration. My space is intentionally
designed to be beautiful and healing.*

November 2023

○ **MONDAY** 13

TUESDAY 14

WEDNESDAY 15

THURSDAY 16

FRIDAY

17

SATURDAY

18

SUNDAY

19

Mandalas are beautiful repeating patterns
drawn inside a circle. They are used
in reflective meditation, so they can
facilitate your ability to reflect on your
own actions—which is what this phase of
the Beaver Moon is calling you to do.

◖ MONDAY   20

TUESDAY   21

WEDNESDAY   22

THURSDAY   23
THANKSGIVING DAY (US)

FRIDAY
NATIVE AMERICAN HERITAGE DAY (US)

24

SATURDAY

25

SUNDAY

26

"Beavers bred in captivity,
inhabiting a concrete pool, will,
if given the timber, fatuously
go through all the motions of
damming an ancestral stream."
—EVELYN WAUGH

December
Cold Moon

December brings many hours of darkness and frigid temperatures. The cold that the Mohawk people encountered during the longest days of winter gave name to this icy moon. It calls us to acknowledge the fire of our spirit. As the moon continues her cycle around the Earth, she becomes a tiny, bright sliver. This is known as her Waning Crescent phase. Just as the moon is preparing to enter her next cycle, so should you. This is a time to rest, recuperate, and ready

WANING CRESCENT MOON RITUAL

It is time for you to rest to bring closure to this moon cycle and prepare for the next cycle. An important component of rest is your ability to dream. Dreams are powerful tools that can assist with guidance and answers.

DREAM FACILITATION STATION

The following three elements facilitate an active dream life.

QUALITY SLEEP: To dream you must sleep deeply. Ensure that your bed is comfortable and your room is dark. Take melatonin according to the package instructions if you struggle with staying asleep. Meditate before bed to help yourself relax. Do not eat anything for three hours before you go to bed so that your sleep is uninterrupted.

INVITING DREAMS: You can invite dreams your way by asking for them out loud or creating a dream list. Add people you would like to interact with or questions you would like to have answered to this list.

CAPTURING YOUR DREAMS: Keep a dream journal, pen, and lamp next to your bed. This way you can access light and something with which to write if you awaken from a remembered dream. Keep a glass of water nearby because dreams can be startling, and a sip of water can gently welcome you back into the physical world. You can reference your dream journal and identify symbols, colors, themes, recurring patterns, and the like. Dive into interpreting your dreams by using books, the internet, or by looking within

December 2023

NOTES	SUNDAY	MONDAY	TUESDAY
	3	4	5
	INTERNATIONAL DAY OF PERSONS WITH DISABILITIES		
	10	11	12
	HUMAN RIGHTS DAY		
	17	18	19
	24	25	26
	CHRISTMAS EVE		
	31		BOXING DAY (UK / CAN / AUS / NZ)
	NEW YEAR'S EVE	CHRISTMAS DAY	KWANZAA

December 2023

WEDNESDAY	THURSDAY	FRIDAY	SATURDAY
		1 WORLD AIDS DAY	2
6	7 HANUKKAH (BEGINS AT SUNDOWN)	8	9
13	14	15	16
20	21 WINTER SOLSTICE	22	23
27	28	29	30

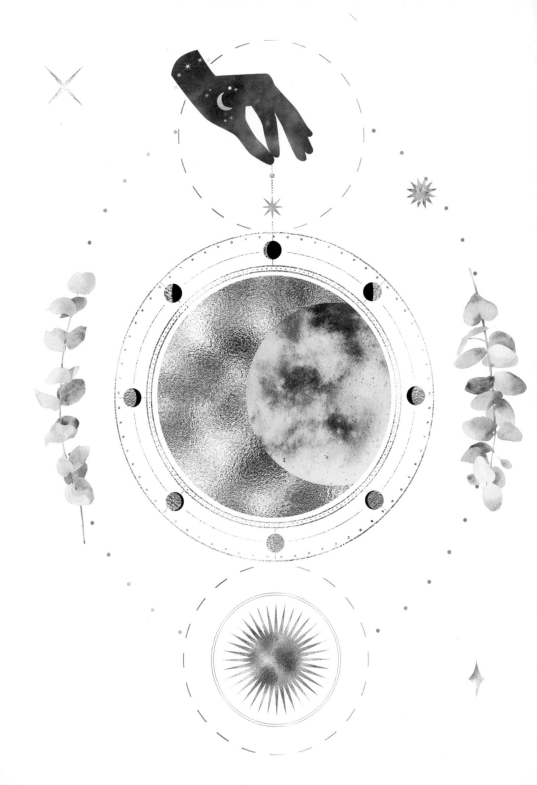

November / December 2023

MONDAY (NOVEMBER) 27

TUESDAY (NOVEMBER) 28

WEDNESDAY (NOVEMBER) 29

THURSDAY (NOVEMBER) 30

FRIDAY
WORLD AIDS DAY
1

SATURDAY 2

SUNDAY
INTERNATIONAL DAY OF PERSONS WITH DISABILITIES
3

December 2023

MONDAY 4

TUESDAY 5

WEDNESDAY 6

THURSDAY 7
HANUKKAH (BEGINS AT SUNDOWN)

FRIDAY

8

SATURDAY

9

SUNDAY
HUMAN RIGHTS DAY

10

Using a lighter or candle speak into the fire,
I am wildly passionate about creating art and
I prioritize making time for creativity. I love
physical movement and nature, so I incorporate
an outdoor activity into each day.

December 2023

MONDAY 11

O **TUESDAY** 12

WEDNESDAY 13

THURSDAY 14

FRIDAY 15

SATURDAY 16

SUNDAY 17

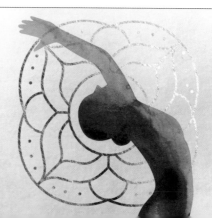

Release the blocks that are stopping you from accessing your internal passion. Repeat the mantra, *I do not let the doubt of others impact me. I do not entertain self-doubt. I am capable and magnificent and I can do anything I want to do.*

December 2023

MONDAY 18

TUESDAY 19

WEDNESDAY 20

THURSDAY 21
WINTER SOLSTICE

FRIDAY
22

SATURDAY
23

SUNDAY
CHRISTMAS EVE
24

"Encouragement is a fire of flame.
It refreshes the soul and revives the spirit."
—LAILAH GIFTY AKITA

MONDAY
CHRISTMAS DAY

25

TUESDAY
**BOXING DAY (UK / CAN / AUS / NZ) /
KWANZA**

26

WEDNESDAY

27

THURSDAY

28

FRIDAY 29

SATURDAY 30

SUNDAY
NEW YEAR'S EVE
31

*I create magic in my life
and the lives of others and
am in sync with the rhythms
of my soul.*

notes

notes

notes

notes

notes

notes

Brimming with creative inspiration, how-to projects, and useful information to enrich your everyday life, quarto.com is a favorite destination for those pursuing their interests and passions.

First published in 2022 by Rock Point, an imprint of The Quarto Group,
142 West 36th Street, 4th Floor, New York, NY 10018, USA
T (212) 779-4972 F (212) 779-6058 www.Quarto.com

Contains content previously published in 2021 as *Living Lunarly* by Rock Point, an imprint of The Quarto Group,
142 West 36th Street, 4th Floor, New York, NY 10018

Rock Point titles are also available at discount for retail, wholesale, promotional, and bulk purchase. For details, contact the Special Sales Manager by email at specialsales@quarto.com or by mail at The Quarto Group, Attn: Special Sales Manager, 100 Cummings Center Suite 265D, Beverly, MA 01915 USA.

10 9 8 7 6 5 4 3 2 1

ISBN: 978-1-63106-892-8

Publisher: Rage Kindelsperger
Creative Director: Laura Drew
Managing Editor: Cara Donaldson
Project Editor: Sara Bonacum
Cover Illustration: Sosha Davis
Interior Design: Chika Azuma
Layout Design: Beth Middleworth

Printed in China

This planner provides general information on various widely known and widely accepted self-care practices. However, it should not be relied upon as recommending or promoting any specific diagnosis or method of treatment for a particular condition, and it is not intended as a substitute for medical advice or for direct diagnosis and treatment of a medical condition by a qualified physician. Readers who have questions about a particular condition, possible treatments for that condition, or possible reactions from the condition or its treatment should consult a physician or other qualified healthcare professional.

All moon phases shown are for the Eastern Time Zone.